Cooking Together

A Book of Recipes

Walt Disney Publications

developed by
Jacqueline A. Ball

recipes by
Sally Lodge

illustrations by
The Al White Studio

special thanks to nutritional consultant
Colleen Marie Grebasch, M.S., R.D.

special thanks also to our terrific and tireless tasters
Amy, Alec and Alison Randall

Twin Books

This edition published in 1990 by Gallery Books, an imprint of W.H. Smith Publishers, Inc., 112
Madison Avenue, New York, NY 10016.
Produced by Twin Books, 15 Sherwood Place, Greenwich, CT 06830
ISBN 0-8317-2348-3   Printed in Spain

GALLERY BOOKS

Contents

A Word to Grownup Kitchen Helpers

With Minnie's help, we have designed this cookbook to be much more than a collection of recipes. The book teaches children important lessons while they are having fun in the kitchen.

The first lesson is that foods that are nutritious can taste good, too. This book emphasizes fresh fruits and vegetables, cheese, whole-grain and enriched flour, cereals, and other nutritious foods. The need to form good eating habits is a lesson that will last a lifetime.

Throughout these pages, Minnie sends another message, about the importance of being a good friend and sharing with others. Children will learn how rewarding it is to work together toward a common goal—particularly when that goal involves mouth-watering treats!

There are other things youngsters will learn as they try these recipes. Without even knowing it, they will be acquiring good work habits and learning to be considerate of others (and of kitchens that belong to others). They will also learn about counting and measuring and about the importance of following directions carefully.

As a grownup helper in the kitchen, remember that there are many potential hazards for children just learning to cook. No child should ever be allowed to use the kitchen without the permission of an adult. In every recipe in this book that requires the use of a knife or other sharp utensil, an electric appliance, a stove or oven, the operations for which a grownup's help is needed are specified under the heading, "Here's What a Grownup Will Do."

There are steps you can take when buying groceries for youngsters to cook with that will make your life easier and promote good eating habits. Before finalizing your grocery list, consider these suggestions:

- Cut down on the amount of time spent supervising children by purchasing packaged cheeses that already have been shredded, vegetables that already have been sliced, etc.

- Search out the healthiest variety of any dairy item or other food that you can find. Whenever possible, buy margarine instead of butter; safflower, corn, olive, and canola oils; nonfat or lowfat yogurt; part-skim cheese; lowfat cottage cheese; 1%-fat or nonfat milk; whole-grain and enriched flour; unsweetened canned fruits; natural peanut butter; tuna packed in water. Two egg whites can be substituted for one whole egg.

A couple of final notes: This book is intended for children who are school age—at least five and six years old. Preschoolers may want to "help," but please be aware that some of the recipes do call for items (such as toothpicks) that could represent a risk to very little children. And last, whatever their ages, be patient with children in the kitchen. There will be spills, and perhaps even a broken bowl, along the way. These mishaps are an unavoidable part of experimenting with cooking. Making a snack or dessert from scratch is a significant accomplishment for children, and it can help to build their self-confidence.

Encourage youngsters in the kitchen and praise their efforts. Your reward may be even better than watching them have fun learning. If you're lucky, they may share some of their creations with you!

Getting Started

Minnie is very excited that you and she are going to spend some time cooking together. She can't wait to share her favorite foods with you. For this cookbook, she has chosen recipes that taste yummy—and are good for you at the same time.

Besides recipes for snacks, meals, and desserts, Minnie wants to share some recipes for special times.

Sometimes Minnie and her friends make things in the kitchen that are not to eat. She will show you some of her recipes for things to play with, like pretend makeup and neat jewelry. It's amazing how many fun things you can make in the kitchen!

But before Minnie shares her recipes with you, she has some very important things to tell you about preparing food. Don't begin any of the recipes until you have read through all the safety and cooking tips. And she wants you to remember: Always ask for a grownup's help when you need it.

Now . . . get ready for fun in the kitchen with Minnie. Before you know it, you will be cooking together . . . Minnie 'n YOU!

Rules for Safe Cooking

- Always ask permission from a grownup before using the kitchen.

- Always ask for a grownup's help if you are using a knife, a grater, a vegetable peeler, an electric mixer, a toaster, or a can opener.

- Wash all fruits and vegetables carefully with cold water before using.

- Plug in all electrical appliances with dry hands. Unplug them as soon as you have finished using them. Hold the plug itself, not the cord, when unplugging.

- Always pick up a knife by the handle, not the blade. When you chop or peel foods, always cut *away* from yourself, and keep the sharp edge of the knife facing away from your hand. Always chop on a cutting board.

Stove and Oven Safety

- Always ask a grownup for help before using a stove or an oven.

- Always use potholders or oven mitts.

- When using the stove, always turn handles of pans *away* from you.

- Hold the pot handle firmly if you are stirring food that is cooking on a stove.

- Set hot pots or pans on a trivet or cutting board, not on the counter or table.

- Remember to turn the oven or stove burners to "Off" when you have finished cooking.

In Case of Emergency

- If you get burned or cut yourself, call a grownup RIGHT AWAY.

- If there is a grease fire in the oven or on the stove, call a grownup RIGHT AWAY. *Do not* pour water on the fire. It should be smothered with salt or baking soda.

Minnie's Tips
for Getting Ready to Cook

- Before beginning to cook, wash your hands and dry them well.

- Roll up your sleeves, put on an apron, and tie back your hair, if it is long.

- Get everything you will need together before starting a recipe. That means measuring cups, bowls, and spoons, as well as the ingredients.

- Read a recipe all the way through before you begin.

Minnie's Tips for Cleaning Up

- Wipe up spills right away.

- Clean up as you go along. Rinse utensils and equipment after you've used them, then place them in warm, soapy water to soak.

- Wash knives, peelers, and graters separately and carefully. Don't soak them with the other utensils, or you may cut yourself when you stick your hands in the water.

- Put ingredients away as soon as you finish using them, especially foods that need to be kept cold.

- Wipe off all counter tops and tables.

- Always leave a kitchen as clean as you found it—or cleaner.

Minnie Says Measure Up

It is important to measure ingredients correctly. Here are some of Minnie's tips.

First of all, always place a sheet of wax paper under the measuring cup or spoon to make cleanup easier.

These are the measuring things you'll need:

- A glass or clear plastic 1- or 2-cup measuring cup (for liquids)

- Measuring cups that hold 1 cup, 1/2 cup, 1/3 cup, and 1/4 cup (for dry ingredients)

- Measuring spoons that hold 1 tablespoon, 1 teaspoon, 1/2 teaspoon, 1/4 teaspoon, and 1/8 teaspoon

Measuring liquids:

- Put the glass or plastic measuring cup down on a flat surface. Slowly pour the liquid into the cup. When you think that the liquid has reached the right measurement mark, crouch down so that you are on eye level with the mark to make sure.

- When you are measuring liquid ingredients in measuring spoons, pour the liquid into the spoon until it reaches the top.

Measuring dry ingredients:

- Use the measuring cup that will hold exactly the right amount of flour, sugar, oatmeal, or other dry ingredient. Place the cup on a flat surface. Carefully spoon the ingredient into the cup until there is a little more in it than the measuring cup can hold. Then use the flat side of a table knife to level it off.

- Do the same thing for measuring dry ingredients in measuring spoons.

Measuring solid ingredients:

- Measure solids such as peanut butter, cottage cheese, or yogurt the same way as dry ingredients. (You may have to press the solid ingredient down into the cup first with the back of a spoon.) Use a rubber scraper to make sure that you remove all the contents from the cup.

- When you are measuring brown sugar, make sure that you press it firmly into the cup.

What Equals What?

3 teaspoons	= 1 tablespoon
4 tablespoons	= 1/4 cup
5 tablespoons + 1 teaspoon	= 1/3 cup
8 tablespoons	= 1/2 cup
16 tablespoons	= 1 cup
1 cup	= 8 ounces
2 cups	= 1 pint
2 pints	= 1 quart
2 quarts	= 1/2 gallon
4 quarts	= 1 gallon

Super Snacks

There are two things that Minnie likes to do best after school and on weekends—have friends over to play, and eat yummy snacks. She thinks the best-tasting snacks are the ones that she and her friends make together.

Remember that good manners are as important when you're eating snacks as they are when you're eating meals. Minnie always tries to keep these things in mind:

- Always be cheerful and considerate of others when you are preparing and eating snacks. Serve your friends first, then yourself.

- Don't eat too quickly. You will enjoy your snack much more if you chew slowly rather than gobble it down.

- Sit down at the table while you're having a snack with friends. Talk about what happened that day at school, or what you plan to do on the weekend.

- Never talk with your mouth full of food, and never interrupt someone else when he or she is talking.

- And, of course, don't forget to clean up after you've finished your snack.

Yummy Peanut-Butter Balls

Makes about 24 Balls

This is one of Minnie's very favorite after-school snacks. She especially likes to make—and eat—these balls with friends. Make sure you wash your hands before you begin, and after you have finished. You will have very sticky fingers!

Did you know that peanut butter was first made in the United States? In 1890, a doctor in St. Louis, Missouri, told his patients to eat peanut butter to stay healthy. Peanut butter is high in protein and contains a good kind of fat.

Here's What You Need:

3/4 cup quick or old-fashioned oats
3/4 cup chunky-style peanut butter
3/4 cup nonfat dry milk
1/2 cup honey
1 teaspoon vanilla
1/8 teaspoon cinnamon
1/2 cup raisins
3/4 cup wheat germ

Here's What You Do:

1. In a large bowl, mix together the oats, peanut butter, nonfat dry milk, honey, vanilla, cinnamon, and raisins. Stir well with a wooden spoon until all the ingredients are well blended.

2. Using your hands, form the mixture into small balls, about the size of whole walnuts.

3. Spread the wheat germ on a dinner plate or a cutting board. Roll each ball in it.

4. Pour big glasses of milk for you and your friends, and roll the balls right into your mouths!

Skinny Minnies

Minnie has named this vegetable snack after . . . guess who! To make a Skinny Minnie, she spreads cream cheese on a celery stick and puts four raisins on top—a crunchy, creamy treat! Skinny Minnies can be made with other veggies, too.

Here's What You Need:

celery sticks
carrot sticks
cucumber slices
cream cheese
peanut butter
chopped peanuts or imitation bacon
   bits
toasted sesame or sunflower seeds
cottage cheese
plain yogurt
cinnamon
raisins

Here's What a Grownup Will Do:

Slice the celery and carrot sticks; cut the cucumber slices.

Here's What You Do:

1. Wash the vegetables. Cut the celery and carrots into 3-inch sticks. Cut the cucumber into slices. Chop the nuts. (Below, see how Minnie the Magician does this without a knife!)

2. Put any of the above ingredients together to make your veggie snacks.

Minnie the Magician chops nuts without a knife. She puts the nuts in a plastic bag. She places the bag on a table, counter, or cutting board. Then she rolls a rolling pin over the bag.

11

Nifty Nachos

Makes 18 Nachos

Minnie likes her nachos plain and simple—just tortilla chips and cheese. But if you like nachos a bit spicier, dribble taco sauce on top of the chips before cooking. Either way, these make a yummy snack.

Here's What You Need:

18 plain tortilla chips
1/2 cup shredded cheddar cheese
2 tablespoons mild taco sauce

Here's What a Grownup Will Do:

Preheat the oven; put the pan in; remove the pan.

Here's What You Do:

1. Preheat the oven to 400 degrees.

2. Arrange the tortilla chips on a metal pie plate. Dribble the taco sauce over the chips, if you like.

3. Sprinkle the chips with the cheese.

4. Put the pie plate into the oven. Cook for 5 minutes, or until the cheese melts.

5. Remove from the oven. Wait at least 1 minute before eating.

Doubly Delicious Dips

Minnie loves snacking on fresh fruit and veggies. Dipping them in these two great dips makes the healthy snacks taste even better. The first dip is for crispy veggies. The second dip is a little bit sweet—perfect for fruit. Mmmm . . . doubly delicious!

Wash all fruits and veggies before slicing.

Dynamite Dilly Dip

Makes 2/3 Cup

Here's What You Need:

1/2 cup cottage cheese
1/4 cup shredded cheddar cheese
2 tablespoons plain yogurt
2 tablespoons mayonnaise
1 teaspoon lemon juice
1/4 teaspoon dill weed
sprinkle of garlic powder
raw vegetables (any kind you like)

Here's What a Grownup Will Do:

Slice the veggies.

Here's What You Do:

1. In a medium-sized bowl, mix together the cottage cheese, shredded cheddar cheese, yogurt, mayonnaise, lemon juice, and dill weed. Add garlic powder.

2. Cut the raw vegetables into strips and sticks, if necessary.

3. Arrange these on a plate, along with cherry tomatoes, pea pods, and any other veggies you like. Happy dipping!

Merry Sunshine Dip
Makes 1/2 Cup

Here's What You Need:

1/2 cup plain yogurt
1 tablespoon unsweetened frozen
  orange-juice concentrate,
  defrosted
1/8 teaspoon cinnamon
1/2 teaspoon honey
fresh fruit (any kind)

Here's What a Grownup Will Do:

Cut the fresh fruit into bite-sized pieces;
open the can of orange-juice concentrate.

Here's What You Do:

1. In a medium-sized bowl, mix together
   the yogurt, orange-juice concentrate,
   cinnamon, and honey until blended.

2. Cut up pieces of apples, pears,
   pineapple, peaches, or any fruit in
   season. Or use whole strawberries.

3. Arrange the fruit on a plate, place the
   plate next to the bowl, and dip away!

Store any leftover dip
in the refrigerator, covered.
The dips will keep
for several days.

14

Munchy, Crunchy Granola

Makes about 4 Cups

This is a snack that your friend Minnie loves with bananas and milk for breakfast, or on top of yogurt or fresh fruit for an after-school treat. Sometimes she packs granola in a plastic bag in her lunch box. Yum!

If stored in a tightly covered container, this crunchy granola will keep for two weeks— if you don't finish it before then!

Here's What You Need:

2 cups quick or old-fashioned oats
3/4 cup Grapenuts cereal or slivered
    almonds
1/3 cup toasted wheat germ
1/2 cup crushed peanuts
1 teaspoon cinnamon
1/2 cup honey
1/4 cup corn oil or safflower oil
1 cup raisins

Here's What a Grownup Will Do:

Crush the peanuts; preheat the oven; put the pan in; remove it.

Here's What You Do:

1. Preheat the oven to 350 degrees.

2. Crush the peanuts (see page 11).

3. In a medium-sized bowl, mix together the oats, Grapenuts cereal or almonds, wheat germ, peanuts, cinnamon, honey, and oil.

4. Spread the mixture on an ungreased jelly-roll pan or cookie sheet.

5. Put the pan into the oven. Cook for 10 minutes.

6. Remove the pan from the oven and stir the granola.

7. Return the pan to the oven and cook for 10 minutes more.

8. Remove the pan from the oven, stir in the raisins, and let the granola cool.

Krispy Krunchies

Makes about 12 Balls

Minnie knows that cheese not only tastes good...it's good *for* you, too. A special ingredient in these cheesy balls makes them crunchy: crispy rice cereal. The easiest way to mix everything up is to use your hands, so make sure they are super clean.

Here's What You Need:

- 1/2 cup shredded Swiss cheese
- 1 tablespoon grated Parmesan cheese
- 1/3 cup whole-wheat flour or enriched white flour
- 3 tablespoons margarine
- 1/2 cup crispy rice cereal

Here's What a Grownup Will Do:

Preheat the oven; put the cookie sheet into the oven and remove it.

Here's What You Do:

1. Preheat the oven to 375 degrees.

2. In a medium-sized bowl, mix together the cheeses, flour, margarine, and cereal.

3. Using your hands, form the mixture into small balls, about the size of whole walnuts. If the mixture is too sticky to work with, coat your fingers with a little extra flour.

4. Place the balls 1 inch apart on an ungreased cookie sheet.

5. Put the cookie sheet into the oven. Bake for 10 minutes.

6. Remove the cookie sheet from the oven. Let the balls cool before eating.

CRACKLE! CRUNCH! CRUNCH! CRACKLE!

Jeweled Fruit Wands

Makes 6 Wands

Minnie loves to dress up in her ruffled pink dress and play fairy princess. When she gets hungry, she makes the perfect princess snack—fruit wands!

Here's What You Need:

pieces of fresh fruit, such as apples, bananas, oranges, pears, peaches, pineapple, or melon
1/2 cup orange or pineapple juice
6 firm plastic straws

Here's What a Grownup Will Do:

Peel and cut the fruit into bite-sized pieces.

Here's What You Do:

1. Wash, peel, and cut the fruit into pieces. The amount of fruit you need depends on the length of your straws.

2. Carefully push each straw through the center of as many fruit "jewels" as you want. Leave room to hold the wand.

3. Pour the juice into a pie plate. When each wand is filled with fruit, coat all sides with the juice. Gently shake off any extra drops.

4. Let each princess wave her wand right into her mouth!

Say "Cheese, Please" Rollups

Minnie makes these a lot. She rolls up a cheese slice by itself, or rolls it around a slice of meat. When she wants to hear a "crunch," she rolls cheese (or meat and cheese) around a celery stick or a carrot stick.

Here's What You Need:

slices of American, Swiss, or
   Provolone cheese
slices of ham or turkey
celery sticks
carrot sticks

Here's What a Grownup Will Do:

Cut up the celery and carrot sticks.

Here's What You Do:

1. Wash the celery and carrots. Cut them into short sticks.

2. Place the cheese slices on a cutting board. Either roll each slice up by itself, or place a piece of meat on top of a cheese slice and roll both up together. If you like, roll the cheese or meat and cheese around a celery or carrot stick.

3. If you don't eat the rollup right away, stick a toothpick through the middle.

Roll these up:
• Swiss cheese, turkey
• Provolone cheese, ham
• American cheese, celery
• Swiss cheese, ham, carrot
Any other great ideas?

Making Meals

For Minnie, meal times are happy times, times to relax around the table and share some quiet talk with her friends. In this chapter, Minnie gives you the recipes for the mealtime foods that she likes best. She also wants to share some tips that will make meals more special.

Minnie's Table-Setting Tips

- Place the dinner plate in front of where the person will sit.
- Put the fork to the left of the plate, the dessert or salad fork to the left of that.
- Fold the napkin and place it to the left of the forks. The open end should face the forks.
- Put the salad plate or bread plate above the forks.
- Place the knife to the right of the plate, blade facing the plate.
- Put the spoon to the right of the knife.
- Place a glass for water or milk above the knife. A cup and saucer belong to the right of the spoon.

Minnie's Very Best Table Manners

- Always wash your hands before coming to the table.
- Offer to help serve the others at the table. Always serve on the left of each person and clear dishes from the right.
- Ask politely for things to be passed to you. Never grab across the table. Remember to say "please" and "thank-you."
- Take small bites and chew with your mouth closed.
- Put your napkin in your lap. Leave it there until you need it to wipe your mouth.
- Ask to be excused before leaving the table. Wait until everyone else has finished before asking.
- Offer to help clear the table and wash the dishes.
- If someone else has cooked the meal, be sure to let him or her know how good it was.

Tuna Melts, All Dressed Up

Makes 4 Sandwiches

Tuna fish and cheese—what a great combination! Minnie likes to dress up her tuna melts with funny faces. Invite some friends over and see who can make the silliest face. Can you think of other ways to make eyes, nose, mouth, and hair? Minnie's choices are on the next page.

Never, ever try to pull a piece of toast or an English muffin out of the toaster with a fork or knife while the toaster is still plugged in. If your muffin gets stuck, ask a grownup for help.

Here's What You Need:

- 2 English muffins, split
- 1 6-1/2-ounce can tuna fish
- 1/4 cup mayonnaise
- 1 teaspoon lemon juice
- 4 slices of American cheese or part-skim mozzarella cheese
- 2 or 3 black or green olives, sliced
- 4 peanuts or 4 raisins
- 4 strips red or green pepper or 4 strips pimiento
- 1/4 cup shredded carrot

Here's What a Grownup Will Do:

Toast the English muffins; open the can of tuna; cut the pepper into strips; shred the carrot; preheat the oven; put the cookie sheet in; remove it.

Here's What You Do:

1. Preheat the oven to 400 degrees.

2. Toast the English muffins in a toaster until lightly browned.

3. Open the can of tuna. Drain it over the sink. Mix together the tuna, mayonnaise, and lemon juice in a small bowl.

4. Cut the pepper into small strips. Shred the carrot. Set aside with the sliced olives.

5. Spoon 1/4 of the tuna mixture on each muffin half. Top each one with one slice of cheese.

6. Place the muffins on an ungreased cookie sheet. Put the sheet into the oven. Cook for 5 minutes, or until the cheese melts.

7. Remove from the oven. Let cool 1 minute before decorating.

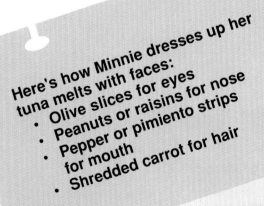

Here's how Minnie dresses up her tuna melts with faces:
- Olive slices for eyes
- Peanuts or raisins for nose
- Pepper or pimiento strips for mouth
- Shredded carrot for hair

Spinning Mini-Pinwheels

Makes 4 Servings

These are great to make when you have a friend, or two, or three, over for lunch, and you don't feel like plain, old sandwiches. You can fill these little pinwheels with just about anything. Have everyone use a different filling, then swap and share.

Here's What You Need:

8 slices enriched white bread or
    whole-wheat bread
peanut butter
jam or jelly
cream cheese
honey
crushed walnuts
cinnamon

Here's What a Grownup Will Do:

Cut the crusts off the bread; slice the pinwheels.

Here's What You Do:

1. Cut the crusts off each piece of bread.

2. Put the bread on a cutting board or other hard surface. With a rolling pin, roll each piece flat, one at a time.

3. Spread each piece of bread with a very *thin* layer of peanut butter or cream cheese. Top with a thin layer of jelly or jam, a dribble of honey, walnuts, or cinnamon.

4. Carefully roll up each layer of bread, like a jelly roll.

5. Slice each roll into 1/2-inch pieces. If the pinwheels do not hold together well, "glue" them closed with a little cream cheese or peanut butter. Spin these pinwheels into your mouth!

Colorful Carrot-Raisin Salad

Makes 6 Servings

The best thing about this salad isn't its pretty color—it's the terrific taste of carrots, raisins, and pineapple all mixed together! Eat it with a sandwich for lunch, as a side salad with dinner, or all by itself for a snack.

Graters are very sharp. Keep fingertips and knuckles out of the way when you grate.

Here's What You Need:

4 carrots
1/2 cup canned, crushed, unsweetened pineapple, drained
1 cup raisins
1/4 cup mayonnaise
1/4 cup plain yogurt

Here's What a Grownup Will Do:

Peel and grate the carrots, cut off the ends; open the can of pineapple.

Here's What You Do:

1. Peel the carrots.

2. Cut off the ends of the carrots. Shred the carrots, one at a time.

3. In a medium-sized bowl, mix together the carrots, crushed pineapple, raisins, mayonnaise, and yogurt.

4. Stir well and spoon into small bowls.

Breezy Tuna Boats

Makes 4 Servings

These sandwiches are a breeze to make—and a breeze to eat. When Minnie is hungry at lunch time, she makes herself a tuna boat. Then she sails it right into her mouth!

Here's What You Need:

- 1 6-1/2-ounce can tuna fish
- 1/2 cup cottage cheese
- 2 tablespoons mayonnaise
- 1 teaspoon lemon juice
- 2 slices American or part-skim mozzarella cheese
- 4 hot-dog buns or soft rolls

Here's What a Grownup Will Do:

Open the can of tuna; cut the rolls if using soft rolls.

Here's What You Do:

1. Open the can of tuna. Drain it over the sink.

2. In a medium-sized bowl, mix together the tuna fish, cottage cheese, mayonnaise, and lemon juice.

3. Spoon 1/4 of the tuna mixture into each hot-dog roll. If you're using soft rolls, cut off each top and scoop out some of the insides to make a pocket. Then fill the pockets with the tuna mixture.

4. Cut each cheese square to make two triangles. Place a toothpick through each. Stick into each boat to make a sail.

Magic Peanut-Butter Tricks

Minnie thinks peanut butter is one of the world's greatest foods. After spreading peanut butter on bread, she adds some secret ingredients, and—like magic—she has an awesome sandwich. She's willing to share some of her peanut butter tricks with you . . . because you're her best friend!

Here's What You Need:

2 slices of bread for each sandwich
2 tablespoons chunky-style or smooth
 peanut butter for each sandwich
any of the ingredients listed below

Here's What a Grownup Will Do:

Peel, chop, slice, shred, or cook any of the ingredients that need it.

Here's What You Do:

1. Before spreading it on the bread, mix 2 tablespoons of peanut butter with 1 teaspoon of orange juice or pineapple juice, or 1 tablespoon of canned crushed pineapple or applesauce. Spread on one slice of bread and cover with the other.

2. Spread 2 tablespoons of peanut butter on one slice of bread. On the second slice, spread about 1 tablespoon of apple butter, honey, marshmallow fluff or any kind of jam, jelly or preserves. Place the two slices of bread together.

3. Spread 2 tablespoons of peanut butter on one slice of bread. Top with 1 tablespoon of one (or more) of these: raisins; crumbled bacon or imitation bacon bits; toasted sesame seeds; shredded carrot; banana slices; toasted wheat germ; sunflower seeds; chopped, dried apricots; apple slices; cinnamon; crushed walnuts or cashews; a slice of fresh pineapple; sliced strawberries. Cover with a second slice of bread—or eat it without a top.

Have-a-Heart Sandwiches

Makes 4 Servings

Hearts and cheese come together in this super sandwich. You may want to double the recipe if you're extra hungry. Minnie thinks you can never have too many hearts!

Here's What You Need:

8 slices enriched white bread or
    whole-wheat bread
2 tablespoons margarine, softened
4 slices American, Swiss, or
    part-skim mozzarella cheese
Heart-shaped cookie cutter

Here's What a Grownup Will Do:

Turn the stove on; supervise the cooking.

The very first sandwich was made back in the 1700s in England. One day, the Fourth Earl of Sandwich was busy playing cards, so he ordered a servant to bring him a piece of meat between two pieces of bread. He ate it while he played on.

Here's What You Do:

1. Place the bread and cheese slices on a cutting board. Using the cookie cutter, cut hearts out of the bread and the cheese.

2. Place each cheese heart between two bread hearts. With a table knife, spread a thin layer of margarine on the outside of each bread heart.

3. Place the heart sandwiches in a skillet and cook on the stove over medium heat for about 5 minutes, or until the bottoms of the hearts are golden brown. Turn the sandwiches over with a spatula and cook for about 2 more minutes, or until the other sides are golden brown.

4. Turn off the burner. Carefully remove the hearts from the skillet with the spatula. Have a heart—or two!

Silly Mouse Salad

Makes 4 Servings

Take a peach half, put ears, eyes, a nose, a mouth, and hair on it, and what do you have? A silly face that you can eat for lunch! Minnie sometimes eats this salad with a sandwich, and sometimes she eats it with a scoop of cottage cheese sprinkled with cinnamon. Either way, it makes lunch time laugh time!

Here's What You Need:

4 large lettuce leaves
4 canned unsweetened peach halves, drained
1 medium-sized apple
1/2 cup grated carrot
8 raisins
4 chocolate chips
16 miniature marshmallows
2 maraschino cherries

Here's What a Grownup Will Do:

Peel, core, and cut up the apple; cut up the cherries; grate the carrot; open the can of peaches.

Here's What You Do:

1. Peel and core the apple. Cut it in half, then cut one of the halves into 8 wedges. Cut each cherry into 4 quarters. Using a grater, shred the carrot.

2. Open the can of peach halves and drain over the sink.

3. Place a lettuce leaf on each of 4 plates. Place a peach half, cut side down, on each lettuce leaf.

4. Make a silly face on the peach, using apple wedges for mouse ears, raisins for eyes, a chocolate chip for a nose, 2 pieces of cherry for a mouth, grated carrot for hair.

5. Put 4 miniature marshmallows underneath the peach to give your mouse a lovely lace collar!

27

Making Sweet Treats

After lunch or dinner, Minnie usually has fruit for dessert, because it is so good for her and it isn't too filling. But every now and then, usually on weekends or when friends are eating over, Minnie will make a sweet treat.

She wants to share these dessert recipes with you for two reasons: They are all super-yummy, and they are all fun to make. When making the recipes, you will have to wait while some of the treats spend time in the oven, refrigerator, or freezer. But that's okay—you will have some extra time to play with your friends until dessert is ready and you can bite into your wonderful creations!

Best Friends Gelatin

Makes 4 Servings

Minnie loves to make jiggly, wiggly gelatin with her best friends. But she loves to eat it more. Minnie uses her heart-shaped cookie cutter to make hearts when the mixture is firm. But cookie cutters of any shape will make this dessert a delight!

Here's What You Need:

2 envelopes unflavored gelatin
2 cups water
1 3-ounce package cherry- or
   strawberry-flavored gelatin
6 ice cubes
1 teaspoon margarine
Heart-shaped cookie cutter (or other
   shapes)

Here's What a Grownup Will Do:

Turn the stove on; supervise the cooking.

Here's What You Do:

1. In a medium-sized bowl, mix together 1 cup of cold water and 2 envelopes of unflavored gelatin. Stir well until the gelatin is dissolved. Set aside.

2. Pour 1 cup of water into a medium-sized saucepan. Cook over high heat on stove until water boils. Very carefully, add the flavored gelatin to the water and stir. Bring to a boil again and remove from heat. Turn the burner off.

3. Pour the cooked gelatin into the bowl with the unflavored gelatin. Stir well. Add 6 ice cubes to the mixture. Stir until the ice melts.

4. Lightly grease an 8-inch square baking pan with the margarine. Pour the gelatin mixture into the pan. Refrigerate for 1 hour, or until it is very firm.

5. Cut the gelatin with cookie cutters. Transfer the hearts to bowls with a spatula. Eat with a spoon—or with your fingers!

Outstanding Ambrosia

Makes 6 Servings

The word "ambrosia" means "heavenly." That's a good word to describe the taste of this great dessert. Minnie has another word that says it all: She thinks this fancy fruit salad is *outstanding*.

The word "coconut" is at least 500 years old. Portuguese explorers sailing around the tip of Africa saw coconuts growing on trees. They had never seen such odd-looking nuts. So they named them "coco," which means "funny face" in Portuguese.

Here's What You Need:

1 medium-sized apple
1 medium-sized orange
1 banana
1 cup canned bite-sized pieces
    unsweetened pineapple, drained
2/3 cup vanilla yogurt
1 tablespoon honey
1/2 cup shredded coconut
1 cup miniature marshmallows

Here's What a Grownup Will Do:

Peel and core the apple; cut the fruit into bite-sized pieces; open pineapple can.

Here's What You Do:

1. Wash all the fruit. Peel and core the apple and cut it into pieces. Peel the orange, divide it into sections, and cut each section in half. Peel the banana and cut it into slices. Place these fruits and the pineapple in a large bowl.

2. In a small bowl, mix together the yogurt and the honey. Pour over the fruit. Add the coconut and the marshmallows, and mix well.

3. Spoon into bowls and dig in.

Top Bananas

Bananas are tops on Minnie's list of best-loved fruits. She thinks these two recipes bring out the very best in a banana. They have real appeal!

Bananasicles

Makes 6 Servings

Here's What You Need:

    3 tablespoons unsweetened cocoa
    2 tablespoons honey
    1/2 teaspoon vanilla
    1 tablespoon milk
    3 firm bananas
    1/2 cup granola or wheat germ
    6 short, thick straws

Here's What a Grownup Will Do:

Cut the bananas.

Here's What You Do:

1. In a medium-sized bowl, mix together the cocoa, honey, vanilla, and milk.

2. Peel the bananas and cut them in half across. Stick a short, firm straw into the thick end of each banana.

3. Roll the bananas in the cocoa mixture. Sprinkle on the granola.

4. Place on a pie plate or dinner plate. Freeze for 2 hours before eating.

Banana Bites

Makes 6 Servings

Here's What You Need:

3 bananas
2 tablespoons wheat germ
1/3 cup crushed peanuts
1/3 cup honey

Here's What a Grownup Will Do:

Cut up the bananas.

Here's What You Do:

1. Peel the bananas, then slice them into 1-inch pieces.

2. Cover a cookie sheet with aluminum foil or wax paper.

3. Crush the peanuts (see page 11). Mix them with the wheat germ and spread the mixture on a dinner plate.

4. Pour the honey into a small bowl. Dip each banana piece in the honey. Then roll it in the nut mixture. Line the bananas up on the cookie sheet.

5. Place the cookie sheet in the freezer for 1 or 2 hours. Eat these while they are still frozen.

Sensational Sleepover

Minnie loves parties, especially sleepovers. She loves to plan delicious treats for her overnight guests, and you can, too. Start with Mini-Minnie Pizzas, and let each guest choose her own topping. Try one of the Popcorn with Pizzazz ideas for a bedtime snack. Eat it while you're sipping on Sleepytime Cocoa. And for breakfast, have your guests help make "Good Morning!" Pancakes—in honor of everyone's best friend, Minnie Mouse.

Mini-Minnie Pizzas

Makes 4 Pizzas

Want to add extra flavor to your pizzas? Top them with
- sliced mushrooms
- onions
- green pepper
- pepperoni
- hot dog pieces

before cooking. Let your friends choose their own toppings. Does anyone like them *all*?

Here's What You Need:

2 English muffins, split
2/3 cup pizza or spaghetti sauce
3/4 cup shredded part-skim mozzarella
cheese

Here's What a Grownup Will Do:

Toast the English muffins; preheat the oven; put the cookie sheet in; remove it.

Here's What You Do:

1. Preheat the oven to 400 degrees.

2. Toast the English muffins in a toaster until lightly browned.

3. Spoon 1/4 of the pizza or spaghetti sauce on each muffin half. Top each one with 1/4 of the mozzarella cheese.

4. Place the muffins on an ungreased cookie sheet. Put the sheet into the oven. Cook for 5 minutes, or until cheese melts.

5. Remove from the oven. Let cool 2 minutes before eating.

Popcorn with Pizzazz

Each Recipe Makes 8 Cups

Here are two ways to make plain popcorn good and sweet, and one great way to make popcorn good and spicy. You can make the plain popcorn any way you like: in a saucepan on top of the stove, in an electric or air popper, or in a microwave corn popper. Just don't eat it all before you pour on the pizzazz!

Here's What a Grownup Will Do:

Make the plain popcorn; melt the margarine and other ingredients.

Peanut Butter and Jelly Popcorn

Here's What You Need:

8 cups plain popped popcorn
2 tablespoons margarine
1 tablespoon creamy peanut butter
1 tablespoon grape jelly

Here's What You Do:

1. Put the popped popcorn in a large bowl.

2. Put the margarine, peanut butter, and jelly in a small saucepan.

3. Cook over low heat until the peanut butter is melted and the mixture is smooth.

4. Pour over the popcorn. Mix well with a large spoon.

Perky Parmesan Popcorn

Here's What You Need:

8 cups plain popped popcorn
2 tablespoons margarine
1/4 cup grated Parmesan cheese

Here's What You Do:

1. Put the popped popcorn in a large bowl.

2. Put the margarine in a small saucepan. Cook over low heat until melted.

3. Pour over the popcorn. Mix well with a large spoon. Sprinkle the Parmesan cheese over the popcorn and mix again.

Sleepytime Cocoa

Makes 4 6-ounce Servings

Here's What You Need:

3 tablespoons sugar
3 tablespoons water
2 tablespoons unsweetened cocoa
3 cups milk

Here's What a Grownup Will Do:

Turn stove on; supervise the cooking and stirring.

Here's What You Do:

1. In a medium-sized saucepan, mix the sugar, water, and cocoa.

2. Over low heat, stir until smooth, about 30 seconds.

3. Add milk to the saucepan. Stir to mix the ingredients. Over low heat, continue stirring until the cocoa is hot, about 3 minutes.

4. Remove from the stove, turn the burner off, and let cool 1 minute before testing.

Pour cocoa into mugs or pretty china teacups for a before-dreamtime treat. While you sip, take turns describing the house you want to live in when you grow up.

"Good Morning!" Pancakes

Makes 4 Servings

Here's What You Need:

1 cup whole-wheat flour
1/2 teaspoon baking soda
1/4 teaspoon cinnamon
1/4 teaspoon salt
1-1/4 cups buttermilk
2 eggs or 4 egg whites
3 tablespoons plus 1 teaspoon corn oil

Here's What a Grownup Will Do:

Turn the stove on; supervise the cooking.

Here's What You Do:

1. In a large bowl, mix together the flour, baking soda, cinnamon, and salt. Set aside.

2. In a medium-sized bowl, mix together with a whisk the buttermilk, eggs, and 3 tablespoons of the oil.

3. Pour the liquid ingredients on top of the dry ingredients. Mix with a wooden spoon until just blended. The batter should be a bit lumpy.

4. Pour 1 teaspoon of oil into a large skillet or griddle. Turn the heat to medium.

5. Measure out 1/4 cup of batter. Pour it into the hot pan to form the mouse "head." Then, taking 1 tablespoon of batter to form *each* mouse "ear," pour them to the upper right and left of the head. Make sure that they attach to the head! Each mouse head will measure about 4" in diameter.

6. Turn the pancakes when bubbles form and begin to pop on top of the pancake. This should take 2 or 3 minutes. After turning, cook pancakes 1-1/2 to 2 minutes on the second side.

7. Carefully remove pancakes from the pan with a spatula. Now you're ready to cook a second batch. Turn the burner off when you're finished.

Minnie thinks nothing beats a little margarine and maple syrup on top of warm pancakes, but give these other toppings a try:
- applesauce and cinnamon
- plain yogurt and fresh strawberries
- a dribble of honey and raisins
- powdered sugar and sliced bananas

Wow! What a way to say "Good morning!"

Birthday Bash

Minnie finds that birthday party games often make her very hungry! Chewy Popcorn Balls make tasty party snacks. Decorated with candles, the Party-Perfect Heart Cake is almost too pretty to cut. (For an extra treat, serve it with lowfat frozen yogurt.) A colorful, fruity drink adds some "punch" to Minnie's birthday-party menu.

Party-Perfect Heart Cake

This great big heart-shaped cake will feed everyone at your party—and you will still have a lot left over. Before you begin, cover a large serving tray or a large piece of cardboard (at least 14 inches square) with aluminum foil, since the finished cake will not fit on a regular cake plate. When the cake has completely cooled, follow the directions for putting the heart together. Then frost the cake with Rich and Creamy Frosting.

Here's What You Need:

1 cup bran-flake cereal
2 cups unsweetened applesauce
2 cups unbleached white flour
2 teaspoons cinnamon
1/2 teaspoon salt
1 teaspoon baking soda
2 teaspoons baking powder
1 cup (2 sticks) plus 2 teaspoons margarine, softened
1-1/2 cups brown sugar
2 eggs
1/2 cup crushed walnuts
1/2 cup raisins

Here's What a Grownup Will Do:

Turn the oven on; put the pans in the oven and remove them from the oven; use the electric mixer; test the cakes for doneness; remove the cakes from the pans; cut the round cake in half.

Here's What You Do:

1. Preheat the oven to 350 degrees.

2. Grease 1 8-inch square baking pan and 1 8-inch round baking pan with 1 teaspoon of margarine each.

3. In a medium-sized bowl, combine the bran-flake cereal and the applesauce. Set aside.

4. In another medium-sized bowl, combine the flour, cinnamon, salt, baking soda, and baking powder. Stir with a fork until blended.

5. In a large bowl, mix the margarine and brown sugar with an electric mixer until the mixture is light and fluffy.

6. Add the eggs to the butter mixture. Blend well, using an electric mixer.

7. Add 1/3 of the applesauce mixture and blend well, using the mixer. Then add 1/3 of the flour mixture and blend again. Repeat this process 2 times, blending well with the mixer after each addition.

8. With a large spoon, stir in the walnuts and raisins.

9. Pour 1/2 of the batter into the round pan, and 1/2 of the batter into the square pan. Do your best to pour exactly the same amount into each pan.

10. Place the pans on the center rack of the preheated oven. Bake for 40 minutes, or until a cake tester comes out clean.

11. Let the cakes cool for 10 minutes. Then, using potholders or oven mitts, remove the cakes from the pans and place them on a rack to cool completely.

How To Make the Heart Shape:

1. On the foil-covered tray, place the square cake with one corner pointing at you.

2. Carefully cut the round cake in half. Place the cut side of each half along the top edges of the square. This will make a heart—ready to frost.

If you'd like your frosting to be pink instead of white, add a drop of red food coloring to the ingredients before mixing.

Rich and Creamy Frosting

Here's What You Need:

1 cup powdered confectioner's sugar
4 tablespoons margarine, softened
4 tablespoons cream cheese, softened
1 teaspoon vanilla

Here's What a Grownup Will Do:

Use the electric mixer.

Here's What You Do:

1. Place the sugar, margarine, cream cheese, and vanilla in a large bowl. Mix well with an electric mixer until smooth.

2. With a dull table knife, carefully spread the frosting over the top and on the sides of the cake.

Chewy Popcorn Balls

Makes 8-10 Popcorn Balls

Here's What You Need:

1/2 cup sugar
1/2 cup light corn syrup
4 tablespoons margarine
1/2 teaspoon salt
8 cups popped popcorn

Here's What a Grownup Will Do:

Pop the popcorn; turn the stove on; supervise the cooking.

Here's What You Do:

1. Place the sugar, light corn syrup, margarine, and salt in a large saucepan. Cook over medium-high heat, stirring constantly, until the mixture reaches a steady simmer.

2. Add the popped popcorn to the saucepan. Cook for several more minutes, stirring, until the popcorn is entirely coated.

3. Remove from the stove and turn the burner off. Let the mixture cool for 5 minutes.

4. Fill a medium-sized bowl with cold water. Dip your hands into the water. Shape the popcorn into balls, about the size of tennis balls.

5. Place the balls on a sheet of wax paper. After they are completely cool, place each in a plastic sandwich bag or wrap individually in plastic wrap.

Pretty Party Punch

Makes 12 6-ounce Servings

Here's What You Need:

4 cups cranberry-raspberry juice or
  plain cranberry juice
2 cups orange juice
2 cups pineapple juice
2 cups seltzer or club soda
1 cup fresh or frozen strawberries

Here's What a Grownup Will Do:

Remove the stems from the strawberries,
if you are using fresh ones.

Here's What You Do:

1. Remove the stems from the berries if
   they are fresh. Rinse them with cold
   water. Put them aside.

2. In a large pitcher or a punch bowl, mix
   together the juices and seltzer or club
   soda.

3. Stir in the strawberries. Add
   2 handfuls of ice cubes if the punch
   isn't cold enough. Pour into cups or
   glasses.

Playing in the Kitchen

Sometimes it's fun to make things in the kitchen that aren't supposed to be eaten. Minnie knows several kitchen crafts that she loves to make when friends come over. These projects are double-fun: they let you have a good time, first when you're making them, and later when you're playing with them! Make sure you have a grownup's okay before starting any of these projects.

Delightful Dough for Playing

There are *so* many things you can make out of this soft dough—Minnie never seems to run out of ideas! Sometimes she uses cookie cutters to make pretend sweets for her dolls. Sometimes she shapes circus animals from the dough, or furniture for her doll house. Make dough in any color that you like. When you're finished playing with it, store the dough in the refrigerator in an airtight container. It will last for a long time. Make a different color every time you follow the recipe, and before long you'll have a rainbow of dough!

Here's What You Need:

1 cup white flour
1/2 cup salt
2 tablespoons vegetable oil
1 teaspoon alum (available at drugstores)
1/3 cup water
food coloring

Here's What You Do:

1. In a large bowl, mix together the flour, salt, vegetable oil, and alum.

2. Pour the water into a 1-cup glass or clear plastic measuring cup. Add about 6 drops of food coloring. If color is not dark enough, add 2-4 more drops.

3. Add the colored water to the other ingredients a little bit at a time. You may need a teaspoon or two more water to get dough to feel right for playing. The dough will lose its oily feeling as you play with it.

This dough is for playing, not for eating!

45

Colorful "Makeup"

Minnie likes to pretend that this is grownup makeup when she plays dress-up with her friends. The recipe makes enough for four different colors of "makeup," but you can change the amounts to make as many shades as you want. After you've mixed up the ingredients, paint your face with paintbrushes or cotton swabs. *Try not to get the "makeup" in your eyes or your mouth—it won't feel or taste very good!* Use soap and water to take this glamorous "makeup" off.

Here's What You Need:

4 teaspoons cornstarch
2 teaspoons water
2 teaspoons cold cream
food coloring

Here's What You Do:

1. Get out 4 small bowls. In *each* bowl, mix together 1 teaspoon cornstarch, 1/2 teaspoon water, and 1/2 teaspoon cold cream.

2. Choose 4 colors you'd like to make, and squeeze 2 drops of each color into one of the bowls. Mix well.

3. You're ready to paint your face—or your friend's face!

Marvelous Macaroni Jewelry

Did you know that you can make elegant necklaces and bracelets right in your own kitchen? It doesn't take long at all. Minnie uses several different kinds of pasta and noodles at once, to make her jewelry extra-special. She makes necklaces and bracelets to match all of her favorite outfits. Do you know what she paints on her jewelry with markers? You guessed it—hearts and bows!

Poster paints can be messy. Before you begin, spread out newspapers on the floor or a table.

Don't cook the macaroni. Don't eat it, either.

Here's What You Need:

several kinds of macaroni or pasta, with hollow centers
string or narrow ribbon
poster paints
markers

Here's What You Do:

1. With the poster paints, paint the macaroni as many colors as you like. If you prefer, you can leave it plain. If painted, let it dry.

2. Very carefully, cut a piece of string or ribbon with scissors. Make it longer than you actually want your necklace or bracelet to be.

3. When the poster paint is dry, you can paint designs or words on the macaroni with the markers.

4. Pull the string or ribbon through the macaroni until it is the right size for your wrist or neck. Do this carefully, so the macaroni doesn't slip off the other end of the string.

5. Tie the two ends of the string together with a double knot and then a bow. Clip off the extra string with scissors —but *first* make sure the jewelry is long enough to fit over your head or hand!

For the Birds

Minnie thinks one of the best things about getting up in the morning is hearing the birds sing! The birds make her happy, so she likes to make *them* happy, too. She makes them this tasty treat and hangs it on a tree in her yard. The birds really appreciate it in the winter, because there's not much food around then. If you don't have a tree nearby, tie the pine cone to a porch or balcony railing or a window box. And remember, this peanut butter is *not* for you to eat. It's for the birds!

Here's What You Need:

a pine cone
a piece of string
2-4 tablespoons peanut butter
1/2 cup birdseed

Here's What You Do:

1. Cut a piece of string long enough to tie to a tree. Tie the string around the pointed end of the pine cone. Ask a grownup to help if this is too hard to do.

2. With a dull table knife, spread the peanut butter all over the pine cone.

3. Pour the birdseed into a pie plate and spread it out. Roll the pine cone in the seed, using your fingers to pat it on.

4. With a grownup's help, tie the pine cone to a tree branch or other place the birds like to feed.